UNBELIEVABLE!

34 AMAZING FACTS ABOUT WEATHER

Mari Schuh

Lerner Publications ◆ Minneapolis

For Ella

Lerner Publications Company
An imprint of Lerner Publishing Group, Inc.
241 First Avenue North
Minneapolis, MN 55401 USA

For reading levels and more information, look up this title at www.lernerbooks.com.

Main body text set in ITC Franklin Gothic Std.
Typeface provided by Adobe Systems.

Editor: Annie Zheng **Designer:** Mary Ross
Lerner team: Cynthia Zemlicka, Sue Marquis

Library of Congress Cataloging-in-Publication Data

The Cataloging-in-Publication Data for *34 Amazing Facts about Weather* is on file at
   the Library of Congress.
ISBN 979-8-7656-0905-7 (lib. bdg.)
ISBN 979-8-7656-2518-7 (pbk.)
ISBN 979-8-7656-1906-3 (epub)

Manufactured in the United States of America
1-1009537-51583-6/15/2023

Table of Contents

COLD, SNOWY WEATHER

Snowstorms happen on cold days.

Snowplow

Small snowstorms last only a few hours.

Blizzards are big snowstorms that can last for many days.

Blizzard winds blow at more than 35 miles (56 km) per hour.

In the US, the Blizzard of 2003 lasted five days.

New York City during the Blizzard of 2003

Some states received up to 40 inches (102 cm) of snow.

Up Next!

STORMY WEATHER.

LOTS OF STORMS

Hail is ice that falls from the sky.

It can be small like peas or big like bowling balls.

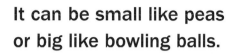

A tornado is a powerful, spinning column of air.

Tornado alley (orange)

The US has the most tornadoes in the world.

Hurricanes are like tornadoes, but they form in the ocean.

Hurricane pictured from space

Hurricane wind ripping a tree out of the ground

When they hit land, lots of rain falls while strong winds blow.

What are the strongest hurricanes to hit the US? Here are the top five in miles per hour (mph)!

Wind Speed at Landfall

1. Labor Day Hurricane (1935) 185 mph (298 kmh)
2. Hurricane Camille (1969) 175 mph (282 kmh)
3. Hurricane Andrew (1992) 165 mph (266 kmh)
4. Hurricane Michael (2018) 160 mph (257 kmh)
5. Hurricane Ian* (2022)   150 mph (241 kmh)

Damaged buildings after Hurricane Ian

*Hurricane Ian is tied with five other hurricanes for fifth place. Stats are accurate through 2022.

Which states have the most tornadoes on average each year? Here are the top five!

1.	Texas	151
2.	Kansas	91
3.	Oklahoma	68
4.	Florida	60
5.	Nebraska	55

Up Next!

WARM WEATHER.

HOT, SUNNY WEATHER

The sun shines brightly on clear days.

Sunlight takes eight
minutes to reach Earth.

The weather can be very
hot for days or weeks.

This is called a heat wave.

Chicago skyline

In 1995, Chicago hit 106°F (41°C).

With humidity, the heat felt like more than 120°F (49°C).

Up Next!

WHAT'S IN THE SKY?

IN THE SKY

Clouds are made of water droplets or ice crystals.

Rain

One cloud can hold billions
of pounds of water.

Most lightning occurs
between or inside clouds.

Lightning can be five times hotter than the sun's surface.

Rainbows happen when sunlight shines through water droplets in the air.

They sometimes
form after rain.

Glossary

blizzard: a long, heavy snowstorm with strong wind

hail: balls of ice made of frozen rain

humidity: dampness in the air

hurricane: a tropical, spinning storm with strong winds

Check It Out!

Bradley, Doug. *20 Things You Didn't Know about Weather.* Buffalo: PowerKids Press, 2023.

Britannica Kids: Weather
https://kids.britannica.com/kids/article/weather/353919

Ducksters: The Science of Weather for Kids
https://www.ducksters.com/science/weather.php

Fraser, Finley. *Summer Weather.* Minneapolis: Bearport, 2023.

Golusky, Jackie. *Weird Weather.* Minneapolis: Lerner Publications, 2024.

National Geographic Kids: 30 Freaky Facts about the Weather!
https://www.natgeokids.com/uk/discover/geography/physical
-geography/30-freaky-facts-about-weather/

Index

Photo Acknowledgments

Marko Korošec/Getty Images, p. 3; deberarr/Getty Images, p. 4; Petro Perutskyi/Shutterstock, p. 5; justkgoomm/Shutterstock, p. 6; Ben McCanna/Portland Press Herald via Getty Images, p. 7; Ron Antonelli/NY Daily News Archive via Getty Images, p. 8; Robert Giroux/Getty Images, p. 9; Gregory_DUBUS/Getty Images, p. 10; tchara/Getty Images, p. 11; mdesigner125/Getty Images, p. 12; Rainer Lesniewski/Getty Images, p. 13; ESA/A.Gerst (CC BY-SA 3.0 IGO), p. 14; Sean Rayford/Getty Images, p. 15; Jeffrey Greenberg/Universal Images Group via Getty Images, p. 16; Francis Lavigne-Theriault/Getty Images, p. 17 (top); Cultura RM Exclusive/ Jason Persoff Stormdoctor/Getty Images, p. 17 (bottom); Peter Cade/ Getty Images, p. 18; Sunrise@dawn Photography/Getty Images, p. 19; digihelion/Getty Images, p. 20; Marc Dufresne/Getty Images, p. 21; Pascal Crapet/Getty Images, p. 22; chuchart duangdaw/Getty Images, p. 23; Jason Edwards/Getty Images, p. 24; Wong Yu Liang/Getty Images, p. 25; Laura Hedien/Getty Images, pp. 26, 27; R A Kearton/Getty Images, p. 28; deberarr/Getty Images, p. 29.

Cover: Marko Korošec/Getty Images.